Pause and Think

Food for the Thoughtmonger in You

Isaac T. Riggins

xulon PRESS

Pause and Think
Food for the Thoughtmonger in You
by Isaac T. Riggins

Printed in the United States of America

ISBN 9781619046399

www.xulonpress.com

Appreciation

I would like to express appreciation to my wife, Gloria, and daughters, Stacey, Alexis, and Maria, who encouraged me to produce this work, and also my mother-in-law, Eva Thomas, and nephew, Marquis Sanders, both of whom told me that I *should* publish this work. I want to thank family friend, Sarita Fahrmann, for encouraging me to publish my thoughts. I would also like to thank the attendees of the weekly

Acquired Knowledge Applied (A.K.A.) meetings, where I am moderator, who urged me on in this endeavor.

Thank you all,

Isaac

Why I Wrote This Book

The motivation and intent of this book of thoughts is to promote *thinking*. Too few people are actually applying thought while proceeding through life. Hopefully as you ingest the contents offered here, you will develop or enhance the habit of thinking.

- Think about what you've been taught.

- Think about what you are being taught.
- Think about what you hear.
- Think about what you see.
- Think about what you say.
- Think about what you *think* about.

We all could live better lives if we would just *pause* and *think*.

Isaac T. Riggins

Pause and Think

1. THE ONLY TIME YOU SHOULD LOOK DOWN ON SOMEONE IS WHEN YOU'RE PICKING THEM UP.

Making light of, talking down to, and belittling others are practices that should not find their way into our being.

If we are wise, we will lift others up, not knowing when we may need a lift.

2. YOU GET THE CHICKEN BY HATCHING THE EGG, NOT BY SMASHING IT.

Not having patience has destroyed what would have been a much brighter future for far too many people who did not allow life to bring to them its pleasures and treasures in due time.

3. THE MAN OF VIRTUE ALWAYS DOES RIGHT—EVEN WHEN NOBODY'S LOOKING.

The person who is right at heart does not need to be supervised or coerced into doing that which is right, good, or fair.

He lives his life in such a way that midnight and noon, Broadway, the alley, and the closet all experience the same person.

4. ONE IS NOT FINISHED WHEN DEFEATED—BUT RATHER WHEN HE QUITS.

As Churchill said, "...never give up."

He who tries one more time every time, wears out the opposition—whatever sort it may be.

5. A TEENAGER/BETWEEN-AGER IS REALLY A GOOD PERSON IN-THE-MAKING.

Many a teen merely needs (and longs for) guidance during those turbulent years.

They need parents/adults to act as rudders for them.

Teens are like ships between shores. They have left the safe shore of childhood and are headed for the glamorous coast of adulthood. Unfortunately, due to the lack of rudders, many are badly damaged by the time they pull into the harbor.

6. GIVE A MAN A FISH—YOU FEED HIM TODAY. GIVE HIM A FISHING LESSON—HE FEEDS HIMSELF TOMORROW. GIVE HIM A CHANCE AND HE'LL FEED YOU.

Giving handouts will break an individual.

Giving handouts will break a family.

Giving handouts will break a nation.

People need to be taught or trained in such a way that they support themselves. In doing so, they in turn are able to contribute to society.

7. WHOEVER SAYS THERE ARE NO OLD FOOLS IS PROBABLY ONE.

Though their chances may seem slimmer than those of the wise, some foolish do manage to accumulate decades on the face of the earth only to get to the end of life and realize they have wasted their time and have not prepared for the hereafter.

8. NEVER START YOUR DAY WITHOUT PRAYER AND WATER.

Use the water for washing and ingest some to aid in digestion.

As for prayer, give thanks that you get to begin this day, and ask for guidance as you go about the day.

9. THE ONLY PEOPLE YOU SHOULD TRY TO GET EVEN WITH ARE THOSE WHO HAVE HELPED YOU. YOU MUST GO IN REVERSE TO GET EVEN WITH THOSE WHO HAVE HURT YOU.

Seek for ways to do good for friend or foe.

To do unto others as you would have them do unto you is to do better unto the one who would hurt you than they would do unto you.

Trying to get even with someone who hurts you belittles you.

10. HE WHO COMPLAINS ABOUT THE WAY THE COOKIE CRUMBLES IS OFTEN THE ONE WHO DROPPED IT.

We put ourselves in most of the circumstances we find ourselves in.

We're usually where we are because of what we decided to do to get there.

11. HAVE A MARRIAGE—NOT JUST A WEDDING.

Is it not foolish to invest so much into a wedding and so little into a marriage?

Think of the money that's poured into a wedding vs. what's poured into a marriage.

We rehearse for weddings. Do we train for marriage? How many other major areas in life do we approach without training of some sort?

Do we really wonder why so many marriages fail???

12. WATCH WHAT YOU PLANT, FOR AT HARVEST TIME IT WILL HAVE MULTIPLIED.

Life can be a pleasing experience or an abundance of regret.

Every sort of seed planted has more in it than one can see at the time of sowing. It is at harvest time that each seed manifests the abundance that was there all the time. If you like your harvest, keep sowing what you're sowing. If you dislike your harvest, change your seed.

13. WE PROBABLY WOULDN'T WORRY ABOUT WHAT PEOPLE THINK OF US IF ONLY WE KNEW HOW SELDOM THEY DO.

There are few people in our lives who deserve the honor of us being concerned about what they think of us.

To some we are a passing thought.

The others are self-centered enough that even if they notice us, they soon forget what it is they noticed.

14. IF WE KEEP OUR DREAMS AWAY FROM THE WISHING WELL, THEY WON'T FALL IN AND BE LOST.

Wishing is not working.

Working brings dreams into reality.

Wishing our dreams will come true is as wasteful as throwing money into a wishing well.

15. A KID WITHOUT DIRECTION WILL SHAME YOU WHILE HE'S YOUNG, AND BE A FOOL WHEN HE'S GROWN.

People/children naturally go astray from that which is good and right, and if left unchecked, they do not contribute positively to society.

Study Psalm 51:5; Psalm 58:3–5; Proverbs 29:15.

16. IF OPPORTUNITY CAME DISGUISED AS TEMPTATION, MANY OF US WOULD OPEN THE DOOR WITHOUT HEARING THE KNOCK.

Opportunity generally shows up as work and has to work its way into our lives.

Temptation merely shows up, and we open the portals.

17. DON'T TRY TO FIT IN. YOU WERE CREATED TO STAND OUT.

You will perform on different stages in life. If you merely try to fit in everywhere you go, there will be no one playing your role.

Life needs you to be you.

18. WHEN MONEY IS WHAT YOU NEED, THERE IS HARDLY A SUBSTITUTE.

Do not make acquiring money the ultimate goal, or the prime reason for your use of energy, but don't apologize for going for more money either.

Figure out whom or what you can turn to when it is evident that money is the need.

19. WEALTH IS POSSESSING THE THINGS MONEY WON'T BUY—A HOME VS. A HOUSE, A GOOD NIGHT'S SLEEP VS. A BED, FRIENDS VS. COMPANIONS, HAPPINESS VS. PLEASURE, PEACE OF MIND VS. A GOOD TIME.

We probably don't realize how wealthy we are because we haven't stopped to take inventory of our blessings.

To sum wealth up as a dollar figure is narrow-minded thinking.

20. FRIENDS ARE RELATIVES BY CHOICE.

We don't get to choose which family we're born into, but we do get to choose whom we spend our time with.

Whom we spend our time with says who we are.

21. ANY DEAD FISH CAN FLOAT DOWNSTREAM.

Show signs of life.

Don't just go with the flow.

There's a reason for you being here. Find it and express it—even if you must swim against the current.

22. GIVE ONE WHAT HE CAN'T FIND ELSEWHERE, AND YOU'LL HAVE A COMPANION.

Meet people at their needs.

If you want more people in your life, find more needs and fill them.

23. IN EVERY REAL MAN THERE IS A CHILD WHO WANTS TO PLAY.

Men, no matter how many decades old, are still fond of certain things and activities—usually more costly by then, but nevertheless thought of fondly.

24. ANYONE WHO HAS STRUGGLED WITH POVERTY KNOWS IT IS EXPENSIVE TO BE POOR.

The one who borrows money to live at a certain level pays more for his lifestyle than he who pays cash for the same lifestyle.

The borrower pays the lender's way through life.

How ironic—the rich are getting richer off the money of the poor.

25. USE NOT THE BRAIN AS A MEMORY BANK ONLY—BUT AS A THOUGHT PROCESSOR.

Memorizing is good. To truly learn is better.

To apply thought to knowledge is superior. It is in such application that we benefit.

A good practice is to write down or record what needs to be remembered—thus freeing up more of the brain for thinking.

26. EACH OF US IS SOMEBODY ELSE TO SOMEBODY.

You won't always be able to say, "this won't happen to me," or "it always happens to somebody else."

Life happens to us all.

Enjoy the good even while you brace yourself for the coming of the not-so-pleasant.

27. MAKE EVERY DAY THANKSGIVING DAY.

Count your blessings every day. You will soon find that you don't have to look hard to find them, and they are numerous.

28. HEAVEN SHOULD BE OUR GOAL, AND IF YOU LIVE RIGHT, IT'LL BE THERE WHEN YOU GET THERE; SO DON'T BE SO HEAVENLY-MINDED THAT YOU ARE OF NO EARTHLY GOOD WHILE YOU'RE HERE.

Be sanctified—not "saintified."

Be holy—not onerous.

Be separated but not distant.

While we're in this world, though not of this world, we are to be close enough to this world to influence the world towards righteousness.

29. THERE CAN BE NO COURAGE WITHOUT FEAR.

Try doing something you don't fear doing. You'll find that you just do it. It's like it just happens.

Try doing something you have reservations about. You'll find that you must dig down into yourself and find a reason for doing—a reason that outweighs the reservations. You may even have to look for self-worthiness to approach the task, along with soliciting support from others.

30. ALL YOU KNOW IS WHAT YOU HAVE LEARNED, AND ALL YOU HAVE LEARNED IS LESS THAN THERE IS TO KNOW.

Never suppose you know everything about anything. Such a position will serve to hinder you from picking up on what you missed earlier.

31. WHEN AT THE CROSSROADS, ALWAYS MAKE THE RIGHT TURN AND KEEP STRAIGHT.

Life often brings people to points of decision. When it's your turn to decide, choose what is right and stick with your choice.

32. THE DIRECTIONS TO HEAVEN ARE SIMPLE—TURN RIGHT AND KEEP STRAIGHT.

Turn from what is wrong. Practice righteousness—and make heaven your home.

33. YOUR CHILDREN MAY NOT LISTEN TO YOU, BUT THEY WILL IMITATE YOU.

If we do one thing and try teaching our children another, we become frustrated assuming our children are refusing to listen to us. The problem is what we are doing speaks so loudly they can't hear what we're saying.

Children learn by example. What are you teaching?

34. THE TRUTH IS CAIN KILLED ABEL—NOT CAN'T KILLED ABLE.

Despite all the naysayers and the can't-be-doners, "able" is still much alive.

We can generally do whatever we apply ourselves to.

35. WHEN YOU THROW DIRT, GUESS WHO'S LOSING GROUND.

Whenever we put someone down, we lose. We lose favor in the eyes of the one we're talking about, and we lose credibility in the eyes of those who hear us.

36. WE ARE TOLD TO HAVE FAITH AND TAUGHT TO BE CAUTIOUS.

Faith is letting go before you can see the easily visible.

Cautious says not to move until you can see where you are going.

By using faith we advance and excel.

Too much caution and we procrastinate, are left behind, and are unfulfilled.

37. DO TODAY WHAT OTHERS WON'T DO—DO TOMORROW WHAT OTHERS CAN'T DO.

Most people won't inconvenience themselves early on to have abundance in a time to come.

Some even choose to have abundance now in such a manner that it inconveniences them in the future.

38. WE ARE OF LITTLE HELP TO THOSE WHO HAVE THE SAME NEEDS WE HAVE.

Two trucks stuck in the mud—what can they do for each other?

Two people broke and in debt—what can they do for each other?

Two cripples fallen, weak, and tired—what can they do for each other?

The message is clear. If you want to help the unfortunate, first stabilize and anchor yourself, then render help to someone else. If you are the unfortunate one (which most of us are at one time or another), and seeking for deliverance, look to a source other than those who are in the same hole you're in.

39. THOSE WHO HATE YOU LOSE UNLESS YOU HATE THEM TOO.

He who hates hurts himself worse than he hurts him who he hates, unless the hated returns the hate.

40. THOSE WHO SAY THE LEAST OFTEN HAVE THE MOST TO SAY.

The person who has little to say often thinks before he speaks—thus raising the quality of his words.

On the other hand, he who utters many words often speaks without thought and without employing listening skills.

41. THE KINGDOM TAKES ON THE PERSONALITY OF THE KING.

Notice the children—you get a picture of the parents.

Notice the congregation—you get a picture of the pastor.

Notice the classroom and students—you get a picture of the teacher.

Take notice of the personality of the school—you get a picture of the principal.

Notice the mind-set of employees—you get a picture of the CEO.

You get the picture. Whoever is head really does lead.

42. ALL OF US LIKE PEOPLE WHO ADMIRE US.

Liking admiration of one's self from another is as human as walking upright.

To hold back admiration handicaps the one holding back more than it does the person he should be admiring.

To admire another is a sign of maturity and causes one to be admired by others.

Want to be liked?—admire.

43. IF YOU WANT TO MAKE FRIENDS, PUT YOURSELF OUT TO DO THINGS FOR OTHERS.

Don't seek friends. You won't find them. Make your own, and you'll have them.

Do for people what others choose not to do.

Do for people what they have trouble doing for themselves.

Lift the lowly and calmly, methodically, and sensitively pull down the thought-to-be mighty. Even he will see you as a friend.

44. LOVE HELPS THOSE WHO CANNOT HELP THEMSELVES.

Love: services rendered without debt attached; deeds done without selfish motives.

It is out of love that we reach out to those incapable of reaching out for themselves.

45. THE EXPRESSIONS WE WEAR ON OUR FACES ARE FAR MORE IMPORTANT THAN THE CLOTHES WE WEAR ON OUR BACKS.

How often do we see fine clothes worn by the same person who wears a smug face? In such a case the facial expression takes away from the clothes and the person in them. The experience is quite the opposite for the person in modest dress and wearing pleasant facial expressions.

46. PEOPLE WHO SMILE TEND TO BE MORE EFFECTIVE IN LIFE.

Just how far can one go with a smile? How much more is accomplished due to a smile? Nobody knows.

Smiling tends to generate a following, while a frown creates distance.

47. IT ISN'T WHAT YOU HAVE OR WHO YOU ARE, OR WHERE YOU ARE, OR WHAT YOU ARE DOING THAT MAKES YOU HAPPY OR UNHAPPY. IT IS WHAT YOU THINK ABOUT IT.

Happiness is an inside job. It matters not what comes your way, or what passes you by, what you grab hold of, or what you miss getting, who comes into your life, or who bypasses you, your degree of happiness is the product of your attitude.

48. YOUR SMILE BRIGHTENS THE LIVES OF THOSE WHO SEE IT.

Let your heart/light shine.

49. A SMILE COSTS NOTHING BUT CREATES MUCH.

Don't be stingy. How much can a smile cost you? How much can one smile benefit you?

How many great friendships started with one smile and are yet to end?

50. A SMILE ENRICHES THOSE WHO RECEIVE IT WITHOUT IMPOVERISHING HIM WHO GIVES IT.

It's not going to hurt. It'll only help. It doesn't take away from. A smile is a free win-win situation.

51. THE ACTUAL SMILE IS ONLY FOR A MOMENT, BUT THE EFFECTS THEREOF CAN LAST A LIFETIME.

It is a small-time investment for lifetime benefits.

52. SMILES, LIKE LOVE, ARE NO GOOD UNTIL GIVEN AWAY.

Try withholding either and no one benefits.

53. NOBODY NEEDS A SMILE AS MUCH AS THOSE WHO HAVE NONE LEFT TO GIVE.

Use the light in your smile to shine on those whose lives are cast in gloom.

54. A PERSON'S NAME IS TO THAT PERSON THE SWEETEST AND MOST IMPORTANT OF SOUNDS.

When you really want to communicate with someone, use their name.

When you really want to impress someone, remember their name.

55. IT IS GOOD TO HAVE SOMEONE WHO LOVES YOU MORE THAN THEY LIKE YOU.

We all need to have someone to be accountable to—someone who will point out our flaws to us. Though it may make us uncomfortable for the moment, ultimately we benefit and grow.

56. ANY FOOL CAN CRITICIZE, CONDEMN, AND COMPLAIN—AND MOST FOOLS DO.

Now that you know who employs these three Cs, go and be wise.

57. A GREAT MAN SHOWS HIS GREATNESS BY THE WAY HE TREATS THE "LITTLE" MAN.

A person's "lack of greatness" does not lessen his humanity, and that entitles him to dignity. The truly great know this.

58. THE DESIRE FOR A FEELING OF IMPORTANCE IS ONE OF THE GREAT DISTINGUISHING DIFFERENCES BETWEEN MAN AND ANIMAL—SO LET'S APPLAUD EACH OTHER.

Let the praises flow. Cause others to genuinely feel wanted, needed, and important. In the process you'll establish your own importance.

Expose the accolades others have received.

One of humankind's most rejected virtues is appreciation.

59. WE OFTEN TAKE OUR SPOUSES FOR GRANTED AND FAIL TO LET THEM KNOW WE APPRECIATE THEM.

Sometimes familiarity blinds us.

Some treat total strangers better than they treat the other half of themselves. How tragic. Where's that stranger when life seems unfair?

Some wrap themselves in their off-spring, not realizing that the kids are only temporary occupants of the home.

Who's going to be there when the kids are gone?

60. DON'T BE AFRAID OF THE ENEMIES WHO ATTACK YOU BUT THE FRIENDS WHO FLATTER YOU.

One can deal with an outright enemy, for by his own tactics, he exposes himself for who he is. But a flattering "friend" may have you buried before you know you are dead.

Flattering is telling someone precisely what he thinks about himself or who he would like to be. We need genuine opinions that others have of us.

61. ALL OF YOUR ASSOCIATES ARE HUMAN BEINGS AND HUNGER FOR APPRECIATION.

Show appreciation. Feed appreciation into the lives of those around you, and when they are full, they will in turn feed back into your life.

62. PEOPLE LIKE TO FEEL LIKE THEY ARE "BUYING IN," NOT BEING "SOLD ON."

Avoid the practice of pushing ideals. Expose/present the facts, but leave the choosing to the listener.

63. MOST PEOPLE GO THROUGH LIFE WITHOUT EVER DISCOVERING HOW THEIR OWN MINDS WORK.

They don't use their minds properly. Too many people don't know what it is to think for themselves. They have been drawn into the practice of following the "leader," whoever that is. "'They' say, we do . . . " Who is "they"? Did "they" even think that just maybe "you" have a mind too? Get acquainted with yourself. Exercise YOUR thinking. You are probably about to pleasantly surprise yourself.

64. WORRYING IS LIKE ROCKING IN A ROCKING CHAIR. YOU EXPEND ENERGY AND GET NOWHERE.

Name one benefit there is to worrying. I can't. So relax.

Expect misfortune. Expect disappointment. Try not to bring them on, but expect them. It's all a part of living in a broken world; and ultimately, it'll be all right.

65. DISCIPLINE YOURSELF OR LIFE WILL DO IT FOR YOU.

The harder you are on yourself, (without going overboard), the easier life is on you.

Do what needs to be done, when it needs to be done, and how it needs to be done, and life yields to you bountifully.

Going for quick and easy usually results in rough and lengthy.

66. IF YOU (BOTH OF YOU) WILL DO AFTER YOU ARE MARRIED WHAT YOU DID BEFORE YOU GOT MARRIED TO GET MARRIED, YOU WILL STAY MARRIED.

How careful we are to put our best foot forward before marriage.

How complacent we have become in presenting ourselves after the wedding.

It is no wonder the relationship cools. We seldom marry the person we dated.

67. ALL THAT I AM, LORD, I AM BECAUSE OF THEE. ALL THAT I'M NOT, LORD, I'M NOT BECAUSE OF ME.

For most of us, God has put more into us than we realize is there.

Unless we purposefully draw out of ourselves what is within us, it is as good as non-existent.

68. IF YOU DON'T DISCIPLINE YOURSELF, SOMEBODY ELSE WILL.

Do what needs to be done without being told it needs doing. And don't do what you ought not do without being told you ought not do it.

It's easier on the ego.

69. THOUGH THOUSANDS MAY DO A WRONG THING, IT IS STILL THE WRONG THING TO DO.

It doesn't matter how many are doing a wrong thing. Multiple wrong-doers never make a wrong thing the right thing to do.

"Everybody is doing it" will always be a lie.

70. SPEND YOUR LIFE LIFTING OTHERS AND NEVER WORRY ABOUT YOURSELF BEING LET DOWN.

Your harvest is the result of the seed you sow. What you make happen for others, God will make happen for you.

Though you may fall low, if you are generally a lifter, you <u>will</u> be lifted up again.

71. DON'T BE FOOLED—MEASURE NOT A MAN'S HORSEPOWER BY HIS EXHAUST.

Notice what a person does—not so much what he/she says they have done, can do, or will do.

72. HE WHO GIVES OUT INFORMATION IS CAPABLE OF TRANSFERRING ERROR.

We live in the information age. Information comes to us from all angles. We see, we hear, we read, and it has become common to draw from the worldwide web of information. But from whatever source we get our information, we should screen it through a mental sifter. There is usually a bit of error, and that part we do not want.

73. BORROWING TOMORROW'S SUNSHINE MEANS TOMORROW WILL BE A LESS-THAN-BRIGHT DAY.

What is for you to enjoy tomorrow is not for you to tamper with today.

When we bring the pleasures of tomorrow into play today, tomorrow has no choice but to be a gloomier day.

Plan for tomorrow. Invest in tomorrow, but don't pull from tomorrow before tomorrow becomes today.

74. SOME WORMS ARE BETTER LEFT CANNED; FOR IF THEY ARE UNCANNED, THEY BECOME SNAKES AND BITE THE ONE WHO LIFTED THE LID.

Be careful what you try to expose about others. Such an exposure may be poisonous to you.

What appear to be mere worms may be baby vipers.

75. YOU CAN'T SELL MUCH OF WHAT YOU ARE NOT SOLD ON.

If you don't believe what you are saying (even about yourself), then don't say it to others. You'll come across as being phony, unreliable, and underdeveloped.

If you don't believe in what you're pushing, you'll hardly have a customer.

76. FILLING THE MIND WITH GOOD LEAVES NO ROOM FOR BAD.

Galatians 5:16 instructs us to "walk by the Spirit"—not "fight with the flesh."

If we would be filled with what the Spirit has to offer (Galatians 5:22–23), we wouldn't have room for the deeds of the flesh (Galatians 5:19–21).

77. OFTEN WHEN WE TALK ABOUT THE MEAN AND UNPLEASANT THINGS DONE BY ANOTHER, WE REVEAL MORE ABOUT OURSELVES THAN WE DO ABOUT THE PERSON WE ARE SPEAKING OF.

A wise person knows that people tend to attempt to point out the dark and dank areas of others in an effort to conceal similar areas in their own lives.

If I can make you look rotten enough, then I won't appear to be as rotten as I am.

Paint an ugly picture of your neighbor, and you won't look as bad.

78. COLUMBUS COULD HAVE TURNED BACK, AND NO ONE WOULD HAVE BLAMED HIM—BUT NO ONE WOULD HAVE REMEMBERED HIM EITHER.

Make your mind up. Set your goals. Go for what you deeply feel within is yours.

There are some things, if you don't do, they won't get done.

There are some things, if you don't do, someone else will, and you will wish that you were credited with them.

Create memories—make history.

79. A SHALLOW-THINKING PERSON IS NOT LIKELY TO MAKE A DEEP IMPRESSION.

Give thought to life, serious thought. Think and rethink, so that when you share in word or deed, what you have to contribute is worthwhile and beneficial.

Become known as one who approaches life headfirst (thinking), not simply headlong.

80. INVEST THE TIME THAT OTHERS SPEND—GET AHEAD DURING THE TIME THAT OTHERS WASTE.

Spent time: time used for immediate gratification.

Invested time: time saved for later use with increased gratification.

Wasted time: time squandered.

Do not worry about tomorrow (Matthew 6:34), but do think about tomorrow while you use today.

81. WITHOUT OPPORTUNITY, ABILITY IS NOTHING.

Along with preparation through education, one should pursue opportunities, and also, one should feel obliged to assist in making a way for another.

82. TIME WILL FLY. IT'S UP TO YOU TO BE THE PILOT OR JUST GO ALONG FOR THE RIDE.

You can focus and direct where your time goes and benefit immensely, or you can just let it go and later wish you had done differently.

83. WAITING FOR PERFECT CONDITIONS, YOU WILL GET NOTHING DONE.

Our world is broken—imperfect—so waiting for perfect conditions to function in an imperfect world is short of logic.

Do what you can with what you have and when you can get it done.

84. STANDING IN THE MIDDLE OF THE ROAD (IN THE STATE OF INDECISION), ONE COULD BE RUN OVER AND RUINED BY THE VERY VEHICLE MEANT TO CARRY HIM TO SUCCESS.

Get on one side or the other.

Focus on one direction or the other.

Wandering around in a state of indecision creates problems for you and others who are trying to negotiate the path you're blocking.

Decide, or someone will decide for you.

85. HE WHO TAKES ADVANTAGE OF THE ADVANTAGE KEEPS THE ADVANTAGE IN HIS FAVOR.

When you have the advantage and it is ethical, use it. If you don't use it, it's just like you don't have it, and you will probably lose it.

Advantages are usually lost to someone more aggressive, and thus are difficult to regain.

86. DON'T BE A WHEELBARROW. IT GOES NO FARTHER THAN IT IS PUSHED.

Have gumption, some get-up-and-go about yourself.

Wait not to be told what to do when you already know what to do.

If you do need a push, develop momentum, so that you keep moving when the pushing ceases.

87. THE WISE MAKES HIS OWN DECISIONS. THE FOOL FOLLOWS PUBLIC OPINION.

Draw from others, but when it comes time for thinking and decision-making, use your own head.

Stake not your head (your thinking) on the opinion poll of the masses.

Dare to expose your individuality. You just might develop a following.

88. WHAT YOU SEE DEPENDS ON WHAT YOU LOOK FOR.

What are you expecting? What you are expecting is what you subject yourself to receiving.

Look for good, and good becomes visible to you. Look for the bad and the negative, and the unpleasant is ever before you.

We see things not as they are but as we are.

Most of what we expect from life, we get.

89. YOUR OPPORTUNITY COULD BE MISSED IF YOU ARE BROADCASTING WHILE YOU SHOULD BE TUNING IN.

Spend more time taking in information than giving it out.

Exercise looking, listening, smelling, and feeling above speaking.

90. WHEN OPPORTUNITY KNOCKS, SOME PEOPLE SEE IT AS AN INTERRUPTION.

Sometimes, in order to take advantage of opportunities presented to us, we must change some of our most thought-out plans and abandon some of our most longstanding desires.

91. DIG WELLS BEFORE YOU ARE THIRSTY, AND PLANT SEEDS BEFORE YOU ARE HUNGRY.

Just as sure as we know that we are going to get hungry and that we are going to get thirsty, we also know that just as sure as we hang around long enough, there are a number of other events that are going to happen to us. Plan. Make preparation for them ahead of time.

Observe the events in the lives of those who are already where you are headed to in life.

Don't let your future arrive before you are ready for it.

92. IF YOU ARE GOOD AT MAKING EXCUSES, YOU ARE NOT GOOD FOR MUCH ELSE.

If you are able to excuse yourself for every mishap in life, you may as well go ahead and excuse yourself from many happy happenings in your life.

We can't learn from the mistakes that we deny or defend.

In life, excuses and progress occupy the same place—but never at the same time. A self-excusing person is not a productive person. A great day in your life is when you realize your problems are your own.

93. IN LIFE WE VENTURE OR WE VEGETATE.

Passivity and productivity both begin with "p" and end with "y." Outside of sharing a few letters of the alphabet, they have nothing in common.

We either purposefully move or we simply meander.

We can't accomplish what we don't attempt.

94. LIKE RUBBERBANDS, WE ARE OF LITTLE USE UNTIL WE ARE STRETCHED.

We do not know what we are capable of until we are pulled out of our relaxed state.

It is unknown to us what we can encompass before being brought to the point of nearly broken.

And once we are stretched, we are forever bigger than we were before the stretching.

95. COWARDS CAN PRAISE CHRIST—BUT ONLY THE COURAGEOUS FOLLOW HIM.

Anyone can behold the deeds of Christ and marvel with great admiration. But to follow Him (to do what He did and what He requires of His followers) takes courage that most of us have to purposefully acquire.

96. WHERE THERE IS PROGRESS, RISK IS PRESENT.

You're hardly going to remain comfortable while moving from where you are to where you would rather be.

Peter risked drowning to walk on the water with Jesus.

Columbus risked "sailing off the edge of the earth" and found more than he bargained for.

At minimum you will risk ridicule in your pursuit of progress.

97. DARE NOT AND YOU WILL SHARE NOT.

If you are not a bit daring, you won't be sharing in the finer things of life.

The harvest of the insecure is meager living.

Bite off more than you can chew. "Playing it safe" creates insecurity.

98. WHEN ONE IS THROUGH CHANGING, HE IS THROUGH.

Because life is constantly changing and change is an inevitable part of living, we cannot choose to not change and yet progress.

Welcome change, but hold on to your values. Procedures do change, but morals are steadfast and worthy of upholding.

99. LET WHAT YOU LEARN OF LIFE GO TO YOUR HEART—NOT YOUR HEAD.

As life reveals her secrets to you, take them to heart. It is out of our hearts that we live our lives.

If we don't let knowledge get beyond our heads and into our hearts, we become prideful of having acquired such knowledge, and we all know that pride sets us up for a fall.

Don't learn just for the sake of knowing.

100. BALANCE IS A VIRTUE, BUT STAY AWAY FROM HER IMMEDIATE NEIGHBORS—APATHY, WEAKNESS, AND OVERDOING.

Be not overdoing in an attempt to get things done, but don't be so laid back that you don't get done what needs doing.

Balance can be found somewhere between stretching without straining and taking a break without quitting, or running without becoming exhausted and walking without loafing.

101. BELIEVING IS SEEING.

When we believe, we do see. It's just that we are not using our natural eyes.

Exercising faith is to see that which is otherwise invisible.

102. TO BELIEVE IS TO DO.

We live out of what we believe.

What we truly believe is exposed by our words and our deeds.

103. THOUSANDS OF WORDS WILL NOT IMPRESS AS WILL ONE DEED.

It is true—action does speak louder than words. Put out fewer words and more action.

Even prayer (talking to God) is no excuse for inaction.

Your life's story is written is action—not in ink.

104. THE DEVIL BRINGS TEMPTATION TO US ALL, BUT THE IDLE TEMPT THE DEVIL.

The devil lurks about waiting for opportunities to ply his trade—temptation and deception.

It is far easier for him to get our attention when we are idling or simply meandering through life than it is when we are properly occupied and productive with our time.

When we become idle, we attract the devil's attention.

105. FEAR CHALLENGED IS FEAR SUBDUED.

As long as you run from or avoid what you are afraid of, you have no control over it. It controls you.

Doing what you must do even while you are afraid to do it conquers fear.

106. SEARCHING FOR EASY WAYS TO MAKE A LIVING WILL WEAR ONE OUT.

Some people expend more energy trying to find the easy way out than they would if they would just apply themselves to something productive.

107. REPUTATIONS AREN'T BUILT ON "I'M GOING TO DO."

Nobody knows what we are going to do, but what we do or have done is there for all to see.

Planning is fine and necessary, but it does not take the place of doing.

108. PEOPLE HAVE MORE HANG-UPS THAN A COAT CLOSET.

Everyone has shortcomings (hang-ups).

Those who have the most trouble with life are those who won't admit to having hang-ups and those who get hung-up on their hang-ups.

109. SOMETIMES WE TRY SO HARD TO BE UNDERSTOOD THAT WE FORGET TO BE UNDERSTANDING.

When we are so wrapped up in our own agenda, we forget that other people have agendas too.

We can easily see that we are "having to" put up with others while not realizing that others are putting up with us.

How often do we try so hard to get others to see our point of view while we ignore theirs?

110. PEOPLE WHO DON'T THINK MUCH OF THEMSELVES WANT YOU TO THINK OF YOURSELF THE WAY THEY THINK OF THEMSELVES—AS CRABS IN A BUCKET.

Crabs in a bucket—If you have only one crab in a bucket, you had better guard your bucket because if that crab can figure a way to the top, it will escape. Put two or three more crabs in that same bucket and you can turn your back on your bucket because if one tries to escape, those on the bottom will grab hold of him and pull him back down. People have the same mentality.

111. YOU HAVE TO BE DIFFERENT BEFORE YOU CAN MAKE A DIFFERENCE.

One cannot be just like "everybody else" and simultaneously help them to improve.

112. LIFE'S BUMPS WILL MAKE YOU BITTER OR BETTER.

It is probably more accurate to say that life's bumps reveal our attitudes—be they good or bad.

113. PEOPLE ARE LIKE WINE. THE GOOD GET BETTER WITH AGE WHILE THE BAD GET WORSE.

There is no automatic gracing with age. We either choose good, or by our choices, prove to be more rotten with the passage of time.

114. IF YOU <u>THINK</u> YOU CAN'T, YOU'RE RIGHT. IF YOU <u>THINK</u> YOU CAN, YOU'RE RIGHT.

We restrict ourselves, and we set ourselves up for successes by the way we view our own capabilities.

115. WOMEN AND CHILDREN COME ON THE SCENE WITH MANY NEEDS, EXPECTATIONS, AND ABILITIES—BUT NO WRITTEN INSTRUCTIONS; MOST MEN ARE TOO ARROGANT TO LISTEN.

Listen, men, with more than your ears but also with your hearts, to the needs, feelings, and attributes of your families, and be the heads you were intended to be in your homes.

And women, please know that it is known that men do not have the market cornered on arrogance.

In general, wives are responsive, making men responsible.

116. THE DEVOURER/DE-VOWER PITCHES HIS TENT AMONG THE MARRIED.

One thing Satan, the devourer/de-vower hates is the institution of marriage. He wishes it would self-destruct, but it won't because God has ordained it. Yet Satan uses any means necessary to disrupt, disfigure, and destroy however many marriages he can. He even starts to work on people's marriages before they meet their spouse-to-be. Marriage is ordained of and promoted by God, therefore qualifying it to be detested by Satan, the devourer/de-vower.

117. OUR CHILDREN ARE TO US LIKE ARROWS ARE TO BOWS.

Our children pass through us, are launched and directed by us for good or evil, depending on who controls <u>us</u>.

118. WHAT YOU <u>THINK</u> YOU KNOW PREVENTS YOU FROM LEARNING.

The human mind assumes that once it "knows" something, it has no more need or capacity to learn that something. So train your mind to accept the fact that you cannot know everything about anything, and in doing so, you will begin to learn many things about everything you encounter. Don't let what you know keep you from finding out what you don't know.

119. BE PASSIONATE ABOUT GOD—WHO IS LIFE.

If we have more passion for anything or anyone else in life besides God, we lose passion for life.

Who loses passion for living other than people who pursue the created rather than the Creator?

120. THERE ARE SO MANY THINGS WE WISH WE HAD DONE YESTERDAY AND YET SO FEW THINGS THAT WE FEEL LIKE DOING TODAY.

Take a look into your yesterdays, and see in them what you could have done to make today a better day, then endeavor to approach today, feel like it or not, in such a way that it makes your tomorrows brighter days.

121. WHAT YOU DO FOR YOURSELF YOU TAKE WITH YOU WHEN YOU LEAVE. WHAT YOU DO FOR OTHERS BECOMES YOUR LIFE STORY.

People are hardly going to remember you for what you have done for yourself, but rather for what you have done for them and others.

122. FOCUS ON GETTING AHEAD WHEN YOU ARE WRONGED. WHEN YOU TRY TO GET EVEN, YOU ARE ACTUALLY FALLING BEHIND.

The result of retaliation is more damage to the retaliator than to the one enduring the retaliation. It becomes hard to distinguish who is wrong. So focus on repositioning yourself to a place where you are less subjected to being wronged rather than focusing on putting someone else in their place.

123. IF YOU DON'T MIND BREAKING THE RULES TO LIVE BY THE LAWS, THE UNIVERSE WILL YIELD ITS BEST TO YOU.

Man's rules/allowances and the laws of God and nature do not always coincide with each other. In such cases, choosing to follow the laws instead of the rules is more beneficial to us.

124. THE GOAL OF "GETTING AHEAD" MAY CONFLICT WITH THE GOAL OF "GETTING ALONG" WITH PEOPLE. AND GETTING ALONG CAN BE A POWERFUL OBJECTIVE. GET AHEAD ANYWAY!

Some of your acquaintances will never agree that you should attempt to get ahead in life, simply because such an endeavor does not interest them, and if you succeed, they fear that they may be made to look bad.

125. PUT YOUR KNOWLEDGE ASIDE—DIVE OFF INTO YOUR IGNORANCE TANK AND COME BACK KNOWING MORE.

None of us know everything about anything. Step away, for a moment, from the things you think you do know and into something you don't know. The benefit is when you return, you will know even more.

126. QUITE OFTEN THE WAY WE LOOK AT SOMETHING PREVENTS US FROM SEEING IT.

What we see in life is often determined by our perspective, our point of view. By broadening one's perspective, one sees things more the way they really are.

127. YOU HAVE POTENTIAL!

Look at yourself—and not at the negatives. Too often when we look at ourselves, we tend to notice the negatives. We all have made some wrong turns, bad decisions, and such, but look at the potential you possess—even the potential you now possess because of the lessons you learned from the wrong turns you made in life.

128. IF YOU ARE TO HAVE WHAT MOST PEOPLE DON'T HAVE, YOU'LL FIRST DO WHAT MOST PEOPLE DON'T DO—AND PROBABLY DO IT DURING THE TIME THAT MOST PEOPLE WASTE.

What we have today is the result of what we did in days gone by. And most people are doing the same things that their neighbors are doing, but they're hoping for a better result, which is hardly going to happen. And one thing people are really good at is wasting time. Become less of a pro at that.

129. WE ARE NOT MERE HUMAN BEINGS. WE ARE SPIRITS EXPERIENCING HUMANITY.

Our humanity is temporary. Our spirituality is eternal. Once we come into existence, we are forever-creatures—just not forever in a human body.

130. DON'T LET LIFE DOLE THINGS OUT TO YOU. LEARN THE COMBINATION TO LIFE'S LOCKER, AND GO IN AND GET WHAT YOU WANT.

Life is governed by laws—laws that are as predictable as the law of gravity. But to the unsuspecting, these laws are as good as safely locked away.

Learning the laws that govern life is like learning the combination to a safe. You can go into it when you want to and come out with what you want.

131. SURE, WE SHOULD NOT BE FOUND GRASPING AT EVERYTHING WE CAN GET OUR HANDS ON, BUT WE SHOULD NOT FIND OURSELVES DOING WITHOUT WHAT GOD WANTS FOR US EITHER.

Grasping at everything remotely in our reach is evidence of greed, and God detests greed. But going after nothing brings one to need. There has to be a balance of taking all that is ours to have while leaving alone what is not.

132. DO YOU GET EXCITED ABOUT GOING HOME? IF NOT, YOU NEED TO CHANGE DESTINATIONS.

If your home is not a place where you are happy to go to, it is the destination that your <u>home</u> is going to that needs changing. It's headed for a wreck and will adversely affect all who are attached to it. Or if your <u>home</u> is fine, check your own personal destination. <u>You</u> may be headed for a wreck.

133. IF GOD IS YOUR FATHER, CALL HOME SOMETIMES.

Pray. God, the Father loves to hear from His children.

134. THINGS ARE SO EASY TO DO—YET SO EASY NOT TO DO. DO THEM AND EXPERIENCE SUCCESS—DO THEM NOT, AND SUCCESS WILL NOT ACCOMPANY YOU.

It's so easy to: commit or not commit, proceed or procrastinate, pray or not pray, eat properly or not eat properly, exercise or not exercise, save money or not save money, make good use of time or waste time.

The list goes on, and the results follow.

135. PREPARE TODAY FOR TOMORROW.

We can't know everything that tomorrow holds, but the condition of tomorrow lies in today's focus. Most people do not realize how much today impacts tomorrow. What we do today does not stop today, but shows up in tomorrow. How can we hope for a fine harvest tomorrow, if we are not sowing good seed today? You can predict the future if you are the creator thereof.

136. GOD KNOWS WE NEED COMPANIONSHIP, AND HE STRENGTHENS US THROUGH OUR FRIENDS (RIGHTLY CHOSEN ONES). SATAN ALSO KNOWS WE NEED COMPANIONSHIP, AND HE WEAKENS US THROUGH OUR FRIENDS (WRONGLY CHOSEN ONES).

Take notice of whom you are befriending, and who is seeking to befriend you. Do a background check on yourself and see whom you have been in cahoots with during different phases and activities of your life. You will likely notice that when you did less-than-honorable things, you were in the company of less-than-honorable individuals. And when you behaved nobly, your companions were of honorable character.

137. LIVING WITH CHANGE IS HARD—LIVING WITHOUT IT IS IMPRACTICAL.

Wherever there is life, there is change; so to resist change is to resist life.

To resist change puts one in position to be left behind.

138. PARENTING IS MORE THAN BEING RESPONSIBLE FOR MAKING BABIES BUT INCLUDES MAKING RESPONSIBLE ADULTS.

There's more to parenting than being reproductive. Bringing the not-responsible and nonproductive to the stage of responsibility and productivity—now that's what parenting is about.

139. COURAGE DOES NOT EXIST IN THE ABSENCE OF FEAR.

Courage and fear often occupy the same person at the same time. Courage is displayed when we choose to do what needs doing even while we are afraid to do it or feel inadequate for the task.

140. PEOPLE WHO HAVE TROUBLE FUNCTIONING IN THE DARK ARE THOSE WHO CAN SEE OR ONCE HAD SIGHT.

People who have been taught the right things to do or have been properly instructed on how to get life to yield its best to them tend to fall harder when they turn a blind eye to their advantage than the person who is less informed.

141. SOMETIMES THE RIGHT WORDS ARE NONE AT ALL.

If anger, anxiety, loss, or even in some cases, excitement is causing your tongue to feel the need to flex, you might do well to bite it.

Ultimately, words have a way of cutting off hearing just as sure as a sword is capable of cutting off an ear.

142. LOVE—IF YOU WANT IT, GIVE IT.

Love has a property equal to that of seeds. If you want to be surrounded by certain kinds of plants, plant those kinds of seeds, and in due time, you'll enjoy the results of your effort. So it is with love. Wherever you plant it, it grows, and in due time, it blesses you.

143. SOME PEOPLE, WHEN THEY WEAR A HAT, HAVE THE GREATER VALUE OF THE HEAD ON THE OUTSIDE.

The practice of thinking is just not a part of many people's lives, and so, they just sort of let their brains/minds vegetate.

Some even think they have thought, simply because an idea came to mind.

Unless one purposefully and regularly thinks, his capacity to think deteriorates.

144. YOU CAN PREDICT TOMORROW IF YOU TAKE NOTICE OF YOUR DEEDS DONE TODAY.

Just as sure as you know what plants will be growing in a garden because you know what was planted there, you can know, (whether you want to accept it or not), what is in your future by your actions of the present.

145. IF YOU ARE READING THIS, YOU ARE HUMAN. IF YOU ARE HUMAN, YOU DO WORSHIP. THE QUESTION IS "WHAT OR WHOM DO YOU WORSHIP?"

What is worship but to feel an adoring reverence or regard for? So, what one highly adores is what one worships—be it a deity, an item, a person, or a position.

We humans were created for worship, and worship we will.

146. IF WHAT YOU SAID AND WHAT I HEARD ARE DIFFERENT, THEN WHAT I HEARD IS WHAT YOU SAID.

People tend to believe their own ears, disregarding what you meant to say, or actually said. So, take care to clearly communicate your intended message.

147. SOMETIMES THE ONLY WAY ONE CAN SAY LESS IS TO KEEP TALKING.

When one runs out of thoughts, he should have already ceased talking.

To keep talking when the thought bank has gone empty is like regurgitating with an empty stomach—you're really sick.

148. YOU CAN PAY ATTENTION OR YOU CAN PAY DEARLY.

There are dues in life. They are simple, but they will be paid.

Be aware of your surroundings, and you won't have to pay so dearly as you pass through life.

149. BEWARE OF THOSE WHO FLATTER YOU AND THOSE WHO WOULD FLATTEN YOU.

The resulting damage can be indistinguishable. Both the flatterer and the flattener are in business for self.

150. GOSSIPING IS LIKE FUSSING. ONE CAN'T DO IT ALONE.

When it comes to idle talk and rumor, if we will hear it out, we are just as guilty as the one who is dishing it out.

The best way to start to stop it is to refuse to hear it.

151. THERE IS SO MUCH THAT I KNEW THAT I'M JUST LEARNING THAT I KNEW.

Some of us are more informed than even we realize we are. Tap into the knowledge already in your possession and experience the benefits thereof.

152. WEALTH OR THE LACK THEREOF IS LARGELY THE RESULT OF HABIT.

When it comes to wealth, we have or we don't have because of our own routine practices. These practices may have been taught to us intentionally or not, but as long as we do them, we can expect the results brought on by them.

153. MARRIAGE IS USUALLY LIKE A LATE NIGHT PHONE CALL. YOU WAKE UP AFTER YOU GET THE RING.

You really don't know what all you're committing to before setting up house with someone. And like the late night phone call, in marriage, once you wake up, you deal with it.

154. THE BIBLE THAT IS FALLING APART PROBABLY BELONGS TO SOMEONE WHO ISN'T.

Whether Christian or not, the quality of our lives can be greatly enhanced by the contents of the Holy Bible. Trying to live life apart from the instructions found therein is, at the least, a recipe for stress.

155. NOT ONLY IS GOD DRAWN TO THE HUMBLE—SO ARE WE.

When was the last time you enjoyed being in the company of someone who thinks more of himself than he should?

156. PRACTICE PUTTING OFF UNTIL TOMORROW, AND YOU'LL DISCOVER THAT YOUR LIFE IS FULL OF A BUNCH OF EMPTY YESTERDAYS.

Procrastinating, and intending to, equal time wasting. Time is the stuff life is made of. You waste enough time, and you waste a life.

157. EVERYONE WHO IS BORN MAKES THE WORLD BETTER. AFTERWARDS, SOME BY CHOICE MAKE IT WORSE.

We all were born for purpose. We have an assignment. We have potential.

None of us showed up by mistake or in the form of junk.

You've got what it takes to make the world better, and it takes what you've got.

158. CONSIDER NOT THE COUNSEL OF "THE COMMITTEE OF THEY."

When you hear that "THEY" said something, ask yourself, "Who is 'THEY'"?

When you figure out who "THEY" is, then analyze the validity of the statement made.

159. APPLY YOURSELF AND SURPRISE YOURSELF.

Most of us are equipped for multiple tasks. We just don't often tap into our wealth of potential. If there's something we haven't done, we just assume it is something we are unable to do. You may be surprised how far from the truth that is.

160. WHEN YOU FALL, FALL FORWARD, AND GET ON YOUR KNEES ON THE WAY UP.

We're all subject to stumble, even fall in the course of life. But when you do, don't give up—get up! And on the way up, pray about the situation. Pray the appropriate prayer—be it for forgiveness, strength, or courage. Pray, get up, and move on.

Even if you fall backwards, roll over and get on your knees on the way up.

161. YOUR BODY IS NOT A GARBAGE CAN, SO WHY PUT JUNK INTO IT?

Our vehicles—constructed of rubber, plastic, and metal—resemble trashcans far more than do our bodies. Yet there are certain things we will not put in or do to our vehicles, while we are careless about what goes into or is done to our bodies.

Taking care of one's body is a small investment with tremendous return.

162. WE CAN HAVE A LOT MORE THAN WE HAVE AND STILL NOT BE RICH.

Richness is defined by more than a sum of money or a collection of things. Satisfaction has to be there. So do peace and contentment. The more of the intangible treasures one has, the richer he is; the potential for stuff-gain also goes up.

163. NEVER DEFEND YOURSELF. YOUR FRIENDS DON'T NEED IT, AND YOUR ENEMIES WON'T BELIEVE IT.

When falsely accused, choose not to be bothered by it. Making a defense is futile. Your friends are already in your corner; and your enemies are not about to change their minds about you.

164. TOMORROW YOU WILL LIVE OUT THE CHOICES OF TODAY.

Enjoy today with tomorrow in mind, for one's present is the stock of his history, and one's history manifests itself in his future.

A productive today makes a sweet tomorrow.

165. GOD IS NOT IN THE BUSINESS OF CALLING THE EQUIPPED. HE MAKES IT HIS BUSINESS TO EQUIP THE CALLED.

You are probably not, in your thinking, qualified for what God has called or will call you to do, but if you will but respond, with obedience, to the call, He will supply you with all that is needed to perform the task. And you will probably notice some who appear to be well equipped but who are left un-called.

This is in no way saying that we should not attempt to prepare ourselves for the call on our lives. Seek, search, and get informed and educated.

166. DON'T STOP AT STRIVING TO ADD YEARS TO YOUR LIFE. WORK AT ADDING LIFE TO YOUR YEARS.

Seeking longevity of life without quality of life is futile. Seek to wisely enjoy your life however long or short it may be; that, in itself, may very well lengthen the number of your years.

Stay out of the ruts that are so common for earthlings. And become a conduit for blessings rather than a reservoir.

167. UNLESS YOU SPEND TIME WITH PEOPLE, YOU DON'T KNOW WHO THEY ARE. UNLESS YOU SPEND TIME WITH PEOPLE, YOU DON'T KNOW WHAT YOUR POTENTIAL IS.

Time spent with people gives you information about them that you won't get otherwise, and it gives you an opportunity to in some way serve them that you probably would have overlooked had you not invested the time.

168. LIFE HAS A GREAT SUPPLY OF SUFFERING, BUT MISERY IS AN OPTION.

We all experience disappointments, hurts, and unscheduled less-than-desirable events from time to time, but if we are miserable, it is by our own choosing. We are recounting only what we don't like and are not counting the many blessings that come our way.

169. WHEN YOU LEARN BETTER, MAKE A NOTE—THEN USE THE NOTES.

We live in an age of copious amounts of information. Our minds are steadily bombarded with the stuff, so we can't trust our memories to hold on to all that is good for us long enough to make the necessary changes for our benefit. So, take notes (and read them), buy books, tapes, CDs, DVDs . . . and use and reuse them to the point that what you're learning is working in your life.

170. AN OPINION IS SOMETHING YOU HOLD. A CONVICTION IS SOMETHING THAT HOLDS YOU.

An opinion rests not on certainty. The word opinion is synonymous with terms such as notion, idea, impression, and view—none of which express certainty.

On the other hand, conviction is what we are certain about—that which has proven to be so. In short, conviction is fixed belief. Conviction will hold when opinion proves to be fickle.

171. IT TAKES A LITTLE PERSON TO BELITTLE.

You cannot be big while you belittle.

It is the immature who attempts to appear mature by attempting to make another appear to be immature.

The mature hopes for and allows for growth in all.

172. YOU ARE WHAT YOU LEND YOUR MIND TO.

We've heard it said, "garbage in, garbage out." What's also true is treasure in, treasure out.

Pay attention to what you introduce into your mind via media, music, association, books, and such; give heed to what you let your mind dwell and meditate on.

173. EVERY TIME WE JUDGE SOMEONE, WE SHED LIGHT ON WHO <u>WE</u> ARE.

We say much about ourselves by what we say or even <u>think</u> about others.

174. GOD TAKES OUR ALL (WHEN WE GIVE IT). AND HE BLESSES ALL HE TAKES.

If your life is empty, it's not because you gave it to God. God never takes what we give Him and leave us without.

175. GIVE YOURSELF A FACELIFT BY KEEPING YOUR CHIN UP.

Close your mouth!

By use of fewer words, we look better in the eyes of many.

176. DON'T JUST GO THROUGH LIFE. GROW THROUGH LIFE!

Every day, through every experience, every one of us can discover potential material for growth, making passing through life without growing a waste.

We all may look back now and then and realize we could have grown more if we'd known more, but please, don't look back and be able to say, "I have not grown in the past 'x' number of years."

177. YOU WON'T BE PREPARED FOR THE TRIALS OR THE BLESSINGS OF TOMORROW IF YOU PUT OFF TODAY WHAT YOU SHOULD BE DOING.

Both trials and blessings form a parade in our lives, but we cannot get the better of either unless we are already in an advantageous position when they show up.

Taking care of what needs to be taken care of today makes tomorrow a better day.

178. TIME IS LIKE A SEED. IT IS REPRODUCED ONLY IF YOU PLAN AND PLANT IT.

Time can be consumed and spent, or it can be allowed to go to waste, or it can be called upon to bring about a desired harvest.

179. A "WOLF IN SHEEP'S CLOTHING" MIGHT STAND A CHANCE UNTIL HE ATTEMPTS TO BLEAT.

Our very speech reveals our character.

180. TO PLACE BLAME FOR A PROBLEM IS A WASTE OF TIME AND IS NO GOOD FOR SOLVING THE PROBLEM.

The most economical thing to do with a problem is to solve it—deal with it. Pointing at it, talking about it, exposing it, giving ownership of it to someone else, or even covering it up will not do away with a problem. It has to be properly dealt with or it remains.

181. THE WORLD YOU AND I LIVE IN RIGHT NOW, ESPECIALLY INCLUDING THE MEDIA (RADIO, NEWSPAPER, AND IN PARTICULAR, TELEVISION), WORKS AGAINST ALL OF OUR BEST EFFORTS TO LIVE A SPIRITUAL LIFE.

Take care as to how much of the world you take in or let become a part of you.

182. YOU CAN CONTROL AND IMPROVE YOUR DESTINY.

Take notice of where you were "yesterday," where you are "today," and where you would like to be "tomorrow," and make the necessary adjustments to get to where you WANT to be.

183. IF YOU GOT THE RESULTS OF THE ACTIONS THAT YOUR THOUGHTS ARE LEADING UP TO, WOULD YOU BE SATISFIED?

Our actions come from what we are thinking, and we reap from what we do. So, if we would monitor our thoughts, we could avoid some actions that would bring forth harvests that we do not desire.

When we deal with our thoughts and attitudes, we govern our actions, which bring about our life's harvests.

184. IF WHAT YOU ARE THINKING RIGHT NOW IS NOT ADVANCING YOU, IT'S TAKING YOU DOWN OR HOLDING YOU BACK.

Our thoughts demand results. The product of the mind (thought) is so powerful it generates results even when the rest of our being is passive.

If my thoughts affect nothing else, or no one else, they affect me—for good or not-so-good.

185. IT IS IMPORTANT TO CONTINUALLY RE-EDUCATE YOURSELF AND EXTEND YOUR UNDERSTANDING INTO NEW AREAS.

When one assumes he knows all he needs to know about any given endeavor, he has just closed the door to any knowledge left available to him on that subject. And please, never stop introducing to your mind things that you are presently ignorant about. This is an ever-open avenue for growth.

186. IF THE THOUGHT IS NOT WORTHY OF WORDS, DO NOT ENGAGE THE MOUTH.

All sorts of thoughts enter our heads. Some are not even ours. They are just passing through. If any thought is not worthy of your speech, do yourself and your companions a favor, and choose to let it flow right on through your head but not out of your mouth.

187. IF LIFE IS PRECIOUS, AND TIME IS LIFE, THEN WHY KILL TIME?

Lollygagging, idling, and procrastinating are all akin to self-murder. Practice them, and your life is simply thrown away.

188. THINK! THINK! IN WHATEVER SITUATION YOU FIND YOURSELF, DO NOT LET THE HEAT OF THE MOMENT COOK YOUR BRAIN.

One of the worst times to be found not thinking is when life seems to have gotten rough on you.

Cool thinking in a heated situation tends to temper things.

Even a moment of heated passion cools in the face of THINKING.

189. THERE IS NO SECRET RECIPE FOR LEARNING TO COMMUNICATE WELL; BUT THERE ARE SOME BASICS THAT CAN BE MASTERED OR MISSED WITH RELATIVE EASE.

Effective communication does not come to be before the language barrier is, at the least, greatly reduced. Learn how whom you are attempting to communicate with communicates.

Great communication involves more than the lower and most forward hole in the head, and if properly used, will greatly enhance our communication skills.

Odors communicate. Body language says much. Listening has become known to be vital to communication.

190. YESTERDAY—SOME DAY. NEITHER OF THESE IS A DAY OF THE WEEK.

Yesterday is gone forever. Some day may show up never. Allow yesterday to be history, get the most you can out of today, and plan your future with specificity—not with vagueness, such as "some day I'll . . ." and remember, putting off until tomorrow sets us up for a life of empty yesterdays.

Today is a down payment on what you get tomorrow.

191. LIFE REALLY DOESN'T END SO SOON. IT'S JUST THAT WE WAIT SO LONG TO BEGIN IT.

You may have heard it said that life starts at age forty. Well, it doesn't have to start so late. What is there about age forty other than we have learned a few things, which, if practiced, will result in a fruitful life? Truth is, we can learn and practice these things at any age and get the same results.

192. THOSE WHO MAKE THE WORST USE OF THEIR TIME ARE THE FIRST TO COMPLAIN ABOUT THEIR LACK OF IT.

Time wasters will attempt to shift the blame to nearly anyone, anything, and anywhere when it becomes clear that they are out of time. Even the clock and calendar are cited as guilty.

193. YOU CAN PREDICT THE FUTURE. MAKE IT HAPPEN.

It's like predicting the fall's harvest because you know what you planted during the spring's sowing.

We know what we did yesterday and what we are doing today, so we know, whether we want to accept it or not, what we have in our future.

194. BEFORE YOU ACT, AND REGRET YOUR ACTIONS, PRACTICE THE THREE PS—PRAY, PRIORITIZE, AND PLAN.

It's hard to go wrong when you invoke God's help with your doings, endeavor to do things in the order in which they should be done, and set goals for achieving.

195. WORK YOUR PLAN, BUT BE FLEXIBLE AND SENSITIVE TO CHANGING REALITIES.

We should work our plans with a follow-through attitude, but also with the realization that adjustments along the way will probably be necessary due to the unforeseen.

196. IT IS AMAZING WHAT AN ORDINARY PERSON CAN DO WHEN PRECONCEIVED NOTIONS ARE ABSENT.

Do not suppose yourself to be so ordinary or bland. You may very well be the seasoning needed to bring the desirable taste to a recipe for life. And view other people in the same light.

197. HAPPINESS IS NEVER DETERMINED BY OUR CIRCUMSTANCES—BUT OUR ATTITUDES.

What we do, who we are, what we have, and how we feel depend upon what we think.

198. TELEVISION IS A KILLER. KILL IT BEFORE IT KILLS YOU AND ALL IN YOUR HOUSEHOLD.

How often do we punch through the remote control finding nothing worth watching, and yet leave the TV on? Kill it—click it off—or it will kill you and yours. What television has to offer is usually as good as medicine or as dangerous as poison—no middle ground.

Television has a reductive suggestion for old and young alike—"Sit down, let your mind go limp, and let ME entertain and inform you."

199. POOR QUALITY, EVEN AT A LOWER PRICE, IS ALWAYS EXPENSIVE.

A product or service of poor quality does not perform its job adequately, and does not last as long as a product of better quality. The cost of poor quality comes in having to compensate for the lack of adequate performance and product replacement.

Pay more at the initial purchase for quality and enjoy the product or service longer without problem, replacement, or reservicing.

200. TRAGEDY STRIKES WHEN LITTLE THINGS GO UNNOTICED UNTIL TOO LATE.

Dams don't just fail in an instant. Neither does a bridge collapse due to the weight of the traffic on it at the time. Dams give way when small leaks and cracks are not repaired early on. And bridges come down because of erosion and corrosion that, if taken care of in a timely manner, could have saved the bridge.

So it is with our lives. A little pain here, a little attitude out of adjustment there, if left unattended, could ruin health and relationships.

201. WE MUST KEEP GETTING BETTER OR WE'RE NO LONGER GOOD.

One must continue to improve or be outpaced by the competition.

Only the mediocre are always at their best, for progress requires that you keep getting better.

Quality is a race without a finish line. And success is getting up one time more than you fell.

Develop your talents, and tomorrow will prove to be productive for you.

202. SUCCESS COMES FROM DOING THE THINGS THAT SUCCESSFUL PEOPLE AND THOSE WHO FAIL DON'T LIKE TO DO.

It does not matter if you do not like a concept that results in success. If you practice it, liking it or not, success is still the reward for doing it.

He who joins successful people, and does what they do, will succeed.

203. ONE OF THE HARDEST THINGS TO LEARN IS THAT OUR WHOLE LIFE IS A FIGHT.

Go ahead and accept the fact that life is tough. If we're going to live meaningful lives, we're going to do it on purpose and with effort. It won't be a stroll in the park.

Expecting life to be easy sets one up for disappointment.

204. EVEN WHEN THE CLOCK STOPS, TIME MOVES ON.

Time moves on—no matter what.

People who accept the fact that time does not respect us, or accept any excuses from us manage well, while those who do not respect time are regularly late or simply left behind.

You can't afford to waste time. That's the stuff life is made of.

205. A MISTAKE MADE IS HUMAN. TO REPEAT IT IS RATHER DUMB.

Every mistake made has a lesson in it. Learn the lesson and be done with that mistake. Miss the lesson, and the mistake or test has to be repeated.

Life really doesn't count us out. It just keeps giving us chances to learn its lessons.

206. IT IS SO EASY TO KEEP DOING WHAT WE HAVE "ALWAYS" DONE EVEN IF IT IS KILLING US.

We should constantly analyze our habits. Enhance the habits and activities that are serving you well. Shake free of the ones that serve to hinder you. Sometimes we don't even like an activity or the results we get from doing it, but change seems to be less enticing than continuing as we are. We are continuously invited to "rut" mentality. Decline the invitation. Purpose to change for the better—even if it gets worse at first.

207. WE ARE ALL SELF-MADE WHEN IT COMES TO WHETHER WE ARE FAILURES OR SUCCESSES.

Sometimes we see a successful person, and we proclaim, "This is a self-made man or woman." Truth is, we are all self-made. The successful succeeds by his own thoughts and activities, and the failure fails due to his own thoughts and activities—SELF-MADE.

208. SOME PEOPLE SEEM TO GET ALL THE BREAKS WHILE THE LESS-THAN-WISE PUT ON THE BRAKES.

Get up and do what needs doing. Do the thing that frees you and abandon those things that freeze you. Take advantage of the breaks in life instead of riding the brakes through life.

209. HE WHO COMPLAINS ABOUT HIS POVERTY RATHER THAN DOING SOMETHING ABOUT IT UNKNOWINGLY CHOOSES TO FAIL.

We can cry about and expose all the reasons for our financial lack, whether we see them as our own doing or that of outside influences, but if we do not forsake the practices that produce lack and take hold of practices that diminish lack, we have simply chosen to remain where we are.

210. WHEN THINGS DON'T GO AS IT SEEMS THEY SHOULD, CHANGE YOURSELF INSTEAD OF THE SCENE.

You may not be able to change things around you and get the results you desire, but you can always make a difference in your favor when you make the necessary personal adjustment.

211. WISDOM LIES ALL AROUND YOU. WHEN YOU FAIL TO PICK UP ON IT, HE WHO CARRIES A BAG OF FOOLISHNESS WILL DUMP THAT ON YOU.

We each have an opportunity to become a bit wiser every day (Proverbs 8). The choice is ours. Both wisdom and foolishness are ever present. And we will, throughout life, be affected by both. If we do not purposefully choose wisdom, the enemy is aggressive enough to sprinkle—even douse us—with foolishness.

You will either pursue that which is wise or be overtaken by foolishness.

212. MY GRANDFATHER HAD A FARM. MY DADDY HAD A GARDEN. I HAVE THE GROCERY STORES. MY KIDS WILL HAVE THE COMPUTER.

Nothing stays the same except our basic needs. How we meet those needs is a cultural thing.

Appreciate the by-gones. They are your foundation. Anticipate the yet-to-comes while you enjoy the present—and experience life at its best.

There is no future in living in the past.

213. WE ARE WARRIORS—NOT WORRIERS.

We must fight our way to accomplishment. Progress does not come to the one who only contemplates and ponders.

214. FIVE YEARS FROM TODAY, WHAT WILL YOU WISH YOU HAD DONE NOW?

Go and do THAT!

215. WHETHER YOU THINK YOU HAVE TO ALWAYS DO A THING, OR THAT YOU ALWAYS HAVE TO DO A THING, YOU'RE WRONG.

You are not the only one who can do any given task. And we only have so much time to get done tasks assigned to us.

216. I AM SHORT OF WHAT I COULD BE BECAUSE OF THE ENEMY, WHO REALLY IS THE INNER ME.

We are limited mainly by our own perspective of ourselves.

217. DEATH WILL NOTICE YOU SOON ENOUGH. DON'T DO THINGS THAT ATTRACT HIS ATTENTION.

Life is short enough, and death is too final to be experimenting and toying with it.

218. TEACH A KID TO LIE FOR YOU, AND SOON HE'LL LIE TO YOU.

Do you ever wonder how many kids are punished for doing what they have been taught to do—lie? It seems okay to lie FOR the parent. ("Momma's not here." or "Daddy is sleeping."), but lying TO the parent gets the kids in trouble.

Teaching kids to lie at all teaches them to lie to all—parents included.

219. LIKE A SPONGE, WE SOAK UP WHATEVER SOLUTION WE FIND OURSELVES IN.

Play in water, and you're wet. Roll in the dust, and you're dirty. Sit around the fire, and you'll smell like smoke. Hang out in the kitchen and you'll smell like food.

So, know that if one lollygags with fools, he turns out foolish, but if he accompanies the wise, he acquires wisdom.

Like a sponge, a mind will soak up whatever solution you put it in.

220. EDUCATION—TEACHERS, PRINCIPALS, ADMINISTRATORS, AND PARENTS, EVEN THOUGH YOU KNOW YOU CAN'T GIVE THEM (THE STUDENTS) ALL THEY NEED, GIVE THEM ALL YOU'VE GOT.

Pour your efforts and resources into the generations that follow you. They will need all that any one of us has to offer and then some.

221. EDUCATION—STUDENTS, YOU WON'T GET IT ALL FROM HOME, YOUR SCHOOL, OR COLLEGE. YOU MUST GO WHEREVER IT IS THAT ALLOWS YOU TO CONTINUE TO ACQUIRE IT.

You are not done with education when you finish high school or college. Make education a continuous endeavor through books, discs, seminars, and the web. People perish or, at the least, do without because of a lack of knowledge.

222. DON'T GIVE ME A HANDOUT, BUT A HAND-OFF—SOMETHING I CAN PASS ON.

Allow me to grasp something that still has use when my race is run—a baton to pass to him who runs his race when mine is finished.

Give me a hand—not a handout. I can use the help—not your sympathy.

223. EVERY EXIT IS AN ENTRANCE.

Exit	Entrance
The Womb	Infancy
Infancy	Toddlerhood

Toddlerhood . . . . Primary Childhood

Primary Childhood . . Adolescence

Adolescence . . . . Adulthood/ Many Opportunities

One Opportunit. . . . . Another Opportunity

Time . . . . Eternity

If we don't perceive the proper timing of the different phases in life, we can malfunction. Each phase in life blends into the next one. Recognizing this, we can enjoy the present while anticipating what's next.

224. DON'T MAKE THE MISTAKE OF THINKING YOU ARE WHATEVER YOUR JOB TITLE SAYS YOU ARE. YOU ARE MORE.

Women, you are more than your job title describes. You are a mom! You are a woman! You are human! That means you are capable of multiple functions. Look inside you. Look around you. You'll find that there's more to excite you than you have previously noticed.

225. DO NOT ASSOCIATE HEFTY WITH HEALTHY.

If one is growing due to exercising, good. Build muscle. But if the growth is the result of a lack of exercising, and/or the intake of too many calories, the heftiness is not healthiness.

226. MAN HAS GIVEN WOMAN REASON NOT TO LISTEN TO HIM. LATELY, ALL SHE'S GOTTEN FROM HIM HAS BEEN LIES, LOUD MUSIC, AND CRYING BABIES.

It is no wonder that women find men to be less than trustworthy these days.

This isn't true of all men, but some men today don't know that one of a woman's needs is to feel secure. And she cannot find security in a sloppy dressing, slack-living, momma-attached boy/man.

227. LIVE HOLY, AS IF THE LORD WILL COME TONIGHT, AND PREPARE AND BUILD AS THOUGH YOU KNOW HE WON'T BE RETURNING IN YOUR LIFETIME.

Live life to its fullest. Enjoy the benefits of living in right standing with God (with anticipation of leaving this world properly), while also enjoying however much time you have left in this present world.

228. TO CHANGE IS NOT HARD. IT'S JUST THAT TO NOT CHANGE IS SO MUCH EASIER.

When one DECIDES that change is necessary, it takes the hard out of the endeavor. And to say to not change is easier is actually misleading; for where change SHOULD take place and is not pursued, life gets harder.

229. IF YOU DON'T TOOT YOUR HORN, YOUR MUSIC WILL GO UNPLAYED.

Do not be ashamed to advertise your strengths and worth.

Find what is yours to do in the time you have to do it, and do it.

230. THE WORLD OF PEOPLE IS LIKE A SHIPPING COMPANY—FAR MORE TRAILERS THAN TRUCKS.

People tend to be pleased with being pulled/dragged around through life—trailers/followers—never realizing their potential for leadership. We are all leaders in some way or another.

231. EVERYONE IS STRUGGLING WITH SOMETHING. MAKE THE BURDEN LIGHTER BY TREATING THEM THE WAY YOU LIKE BEING TREATED.

Be merciful and considerate. Treat everybody as though you know they have a problem in life. Because they do.

232. MAYBE YOU DID TURN OVER A NEW LEAF; BUT DID IT FALL FROM THE SAME TREE?

Be not superficial in your resolves. Dig deep. Get to the root of matters of importance in life. You may even need to camp out under a new tree—relocate.

233. WHEN CHOOSING A PARTNER, DON'T BE SO INTO THE PACKAGE THAT YOU FAIL TO NOTICE THE CONTENTS THEREOF.

Look beyond looks.

Appearances can hide both treasure and trash.

Take the time to open the package and investigate what's behind the façade.

234. YOUR EARS ARE INTAKE VALVES, TAKING IN MIND FUEL WHICH RUNS OR RUINS YOUR LIFE.

As careful as we are about the quality of fuel we run through our auto engines, we should be more careful about the quality of fuel we run our minds on.

235. HE WHO THINKS THANKS.

If we would just apply a little thought, each of us could find something to give thanks for. And if we REALLY did some thinking, we might even rejoice.

It is the person who doesn't think, or whose focus is off, who doesn't give thanks.

236. "MISS DIRECTED"—SHE'LL TAKE YOU AROUND THE SIDE, OUT THE BACK, AND OVER THE HILLS, BUT WITH HER, YOU'LL NEVER COME INTO SUCCESS.

Stay away from misdirection. It'll never get you where you want to be when you want to be there.

237. THINK RIGHT TOWARD YOURSELF; THINK RIGHT TOWARD OTHER PEOPLE, AND GO FOR IT—GO FAR.

Get your thinking right, and as you proceed through life, you may go farther than even you had anticipated.

238. OPPOSITION AND TEMPTATION WILL ALWAYS BE PRESENT. DO THE RIGHT THING.

Make plans to do that which is right, and stick to your plans.

239. MOST PEOPLE KNOW SO MUCH THAT THEY CAN'T LEARN WHAT THEY DON'T KNOW.

Knowledge tends to bring with it an arrogance that often blocks out what could be added knowledge.

Once people know SOMETHING, some think they know everything, or at the least, enough to no longer need to be attentive.

240. SOME PEOPLE KNOW THE PRICE OF MANY THINGS AND THE VALUE OF FEW, IF ANY.

The worth of an item cannot be assessed by its price tag. The merchant's code is, "How much can I get for it?" not, "How much do I have in it?" And certainly not, "How much use will it be to the customer?"

241. IT PAYS TO THINK QUALITY WHILE IT COSTS TO THINK QUANTITY.

Having more does not favorably compare with quality. Choosing quality over quantity cuts down on clutter, makes us more efficient, and saves us financially. We generally do not have to replace as often when we choose quality products.

Trying to get as many as you can of an item at the lowest price is often an act of ripping off oneself.

242. PEOPLE—WE ARE MORE ALIKE THAN WE ARE DIFFERENT.

While we each are different in our own ways, we are very much alike in a variety of ways. We all like and/or need affirmation, acceptance, and some degree of comfort.

Our ultimate goals and demands of life are basically the same, though our approaches to achieve them may differ due to personality differences and life experiences.

243. LIFE IS TOO SHORT TO SPEND IT WITH A LONG FACE.

Cheer up today! If you don't do so soon, you just may spend the rest of your life in gloom. Who wants that?

244. ONE MINISTERS OUT OF WHAT ONE IS.

We are the sum total of our life experiences so far. This is what determines what service we are to others.

245. IF YOU SLEEP WITH DOGS, YOU'RE SUBJECT TO WAKE UP IN A PILE O' TICKS/POLITICS.

Watch; take notice of whom you spend your time with. It'll have an effect on whose back you scratch, and whom you'll call on when your back needs scratching.

246. FREEDOM COMES WITH UNDERSTANDING WHO YOU ARE.

When you know who you are, you have no real need to impress.

Knowing yourself well enough to recognize your strengths and your weaknesses, what you can contribute and your limitations, you are free to focus on impacting the world instead of impressing.

247. BY THE TIME MOST PEOPLE FINISH SCHOOL, THEY ARE SO USED TO BEING DISCIPLINED BY OTHERS, THEY CAN'T DISCIPLINE THEMSELVES. DON'T BE ONE OF THE "MOST."

Few learn the discipline of disciplining themselves. Most people go through their whole earthly existence expecting to be told when to be where and what to do while there.

Learn to tell YOURSELF what you will do and what you won't do, where you will go and where you won't.

248. JESUS LED A BALANCED LIFE. HE LISTENED, AND HE SPOKE. HE CRIED AND LAUGHED. HE SPENT TIME ALONE, YET HE ENJOYED COMPANY. IN SOME INSTANCES HE ACTED QUICKLY, BUT AT OTHER TIMES HE ALLOWED TIME TO PASS.

Be a real Christian. Live like Jesus. Too many believe that Christian living is spiritualizing every facet of life, or living a life of mock humility, and of as little pleasure as one can get by with.

If you're going to be a Christian, study the Christ! And learn that He did nothing in excess, and neither did He attempt to impress.

249. WHAT WOULD IT PROFIT A MAN OR WOMAN TO GAIN THE WHOLE WORLD AND LOSE HIS/ HER CHILDREN'S SOULS?

Why run the risk of losing or misguiding your children while you chose fame or fortune. There is more pleasure in gaining your children at the expense of fortune than there is in gaining fortune at the expense of your children.

Relationship between parent and child usually goes sour due to lacking on the part of the parent. Our children look to us expecting. When they don't get what's needed, it is then that they look elsewhere.

250. IF YOU WANT TO BE COOL, BE YOURSELF. WHEN YOU IMITATE OTHERS, YOU CHANGE THE "C" INTO AN "F."

Trying to make a reputation for yourself by being like someone else is simply the work of a fool—not one destined to be cool.

251. MONEY OR THE LACK THEREOF CAN BE USED AS A MOTIVATOR OR STEPPING STONE, AS A BRIDGE FROM WHERE YOU ARE TO WHERE YOU WANT TO BE.

The proper use of funds on hand and the proper attitude toward the recognition of and response to lack are alike in that either can build a solid bridge to take you from where you are to where you would rather be.

252. LIFE IS EITHER AN EXPERIENCE OF PRAYER OR AN EXPERIENCE OF PRESSURE.

Although life is demanding, we who commune with God on a regular basis are less pressured by life's demands than those who don't have that practice, but anyone can develop this relationship, for God wills it for all.

253. DO TODAY WHAT YOU DON'T WANT TO FIND UNDONE TOMORROW.

Why procrastinate? "Going to do" is the same as not doing.

What needs to be done will need to be done until it's done.

254. THINK OF WHAT DOES NOT CROSS THE MINDS OF THE MASSES.

There are ideas that come to your mind but do not approach the minds of many. Contemplate those matters. They just may be your ticket to your greater desires.

Think about your actions of yesterday and how they affect your life today, and contemplate your actions of today in search of how they will impact your future.

255. AN EDUCATION WILL ALWAYS COST SOMETHING, BUT IGNORANCE WILL COST MORE.

The learning process will always cost you something—time, money, an inconvenience. Pay it, and get on with life. If you remain ignorant, you might pay for the rest of your life or literally with your life.

256. NO MATTER WHAT YOU KNOW, ALWAYS KNOW THAT THERE IS MORE TO KNOW.

Keep reminding yourself that you do not know all there is to know about ANYTHING.

You don't know what you don't know—sometimes to the point that you don't know the right questions to ask to learn what you don't know.

257. FRIENDS ARE LIKE ELEVATORS. THEY TAKE US UP, OR THEY TAKE US DOWN. WE CHOOSE.

Some friends prompt us to rise to new heights. Others seek to drag us to the pits. We choose which ride we take.

Associate with people who are going up, or those who you do associate with will aid in bringing you down.

258. WHEN CRITICIZED, THINK, AND YOU'LL THANK.

When you THINK in the wake of criticism, you may become thankful that you are better informed than the person who is criticizing, or you may become thankful that your critic has pointed out a genuine flaw of yours.

259. THE SMALL MIND IS OFTEN EXPOSED BY THE BIG MOUTH.

So often a small mind could remain concealed or inconspicuous if words would be restrained.

260. WHEN SATAN TRIES TO REMIND YOU OF YOUR PAST, JUST REMIND HIM OF HIS FUTURE.

You know where you've been, and you're through with it. Satan knows where he's going, and he dreads it.

261. IN DEALING WITH YOUR ADVERSARY, ALWAYS DOUBT THAT HE'S WITHOUT ANOTHER WEAPON, AND NEVER SUPPOSE HE'S TOTALLY EXPOSED.

Fight with all your might, all your resources, and with all your wits, or concede to losing the battle.

262. SOME PEOPLE ARE LIKE BROOKS: THEY DRY UP (AND LEAVE) WHEN THEY'RE MOST NEEDED.

You cannot always count on people to be there when you need them. Some will prove to have the same needs you have. Therefore they can't help you. Others will just disappear.

263. NEVER LET ANOTHER'S LIMIT BE YOUR LEVEL.

Do not stop where others are when they reach their limit, and always remember that no one else knows you well enough to dictate to you when you have reached your limit.

264. PEOPLE ARE LIKE FOOD—GOOD ONLY FOR SO LONG. MAKE YOURSELF PALATABLE FOR GOOD USE, OR YOU'LL BECOME DISTASTEFUL AND GET DISCARDED.

Be good where you are, while you're there, and to as many as care to have a taste of you. Even so, no matter how wonderful and helpful we may be, soon enough our usefulness expires and we pass on.

265. THE TRAFFIC ON ADVICE AVENUE FLOWS BOTH WAYS.

If one likes giving advice, it only makes sense to appreciate taking advice too. For when you take advice, you have more advice to share in times to come.

CPSIA information can be obtained at www.ICGtesting.com
Printed in the USA
LVOW062235010212

266672LV00002B/3/P

9 781619 046399